3

Common Core State Standards

Third Grade Assessments

Grade 3

- **Math Standards**
- **English Standards**

Worksheets and Activities that teach every standard!

Table of Contents

Use your mouse to navigate through the workbook by clicking on the Standard.

3

Common Core State Standards

English Assessments

Grade 3

- **Math Standards**
- **English Standards**

Worksheets and Activities that teach every standard!

Name: _____ **Date:** _____

Directions: Choose a grade-level text to read. Ask 3 questions that can be answered by reading the text. Provide responses to the questions, citing evidence from the text.

Assessment

Text: _____

Author: _____

Q 1: _____

_____

A 1: _____

_____

Q 2: _____

_____

A 2: _____

_____

Q 3: _____

_____

A 3: _____

_____

Name: _____ **Date:** _____

Directions: Read the folktale below. Determine the central message and explain how it is conveyed through key details in the text.

Assessment - Page 1

The Ant and the Grasshopper

Once there lived an ant and a grasshopper in a grassy meadow.

All day long the ant would work hard, collecting grains of wheat from the farmer's field far away. She would hurry to the field every morning, as soon as it was light enough to see by, and toil back with a heavy grain of wheat balanced on her head. She would put the grain of wheat carefully away in her larder, and then hurry back to the field for another one. All day long she would work, without stop or rest, scurrying back and forth from the field, collecting the grains of wheat and storing them carefully in her larder.

The grasshopper would look at her and laugh. 'Why do you work so hard, dear ant?' he would say. 'Come, rest awhile, listen to my song. Summer is here, the days are long and bright. Why waste the sunshine in labour and toil?'

The ant would ignore him, and head bent, would just hurry to the field a little faster. This would make the grasshopper laugh even louder. 'What a silly little ant you are!' he would call after her. 'Come, come and dance with me! Forget about work! Enjoy the summer! Live a little!' And the grasshopper would hop away across the meadow, singing and dancing merrily.

Summer faded into autumn, and autumn turned into winter. The sun was hardly seen, and the days were short and grey, the nights long and dark. It became freezing cold, and snow began to fall.

The grasshopper didn't feel like singing any more. He was cold and hungry. He had nowhere to shelter from the snow, and nothing to eat. The meadow and the farmer's field were covered in snow, and there was no food to be had. 'Oh what shall I do? Where shall I go?' wailed the grasshopper. Suddenly he remembered the ant. 'Ah - I shall go to the ant and ask her for food and shelter!' declared the grasshopper, perking up. So off he went to the ant's house and knocked at her door. 'Hello ant!' he cried cheerfully. 'Here I am, to sing for you, as I warm myself by your fire, while you get me some food from that larder of yours!'

The ant looked at the grasshopper and said, 'All summer long I worked hard while you made fun of me, and sang and danced. You should have thought of winter then! Find somewhere else to sing, grasshopper! There is no warmth or food for you here!' And the ant shut the door in the grasshopper's face.

It is wise to worry about tomorrow today.

Name:_____   **Date:** _____

Directions: Read a folktale, fable, or myth. Determine the central message and explain how it is conveyed through key details in the text.

Assessment - Page 2

Title: _____

The central message of this story is: _____

_____

_____

Key details that support the central message: _____

_____

_____

_____

_____

_____

_____

_____

_____

_____

_____

Name:_____ **Date:**_____

Directions: Choose a character from a piece of fiction writing. Describe the character in detail. Explain how the character's actions contribute to an event in the story.

Assessment

Title:_____

Author:_____

Character: _____

Description:_____

_____

_____

_____

Event:_____

_____

_____

_____

_____

Character's Action:_____

_____

_____

_____

Character's Contribution:_____

_____

_____

_____

Name:_____   **Date:**_____

Directions: Read the story provided. Find examples of nonliteral, or figurative, language used within the story. Write the examples, then, rewrite them in literal language. Make sure the meaning stays the same.

Assessment

Title:_____

Author:_____

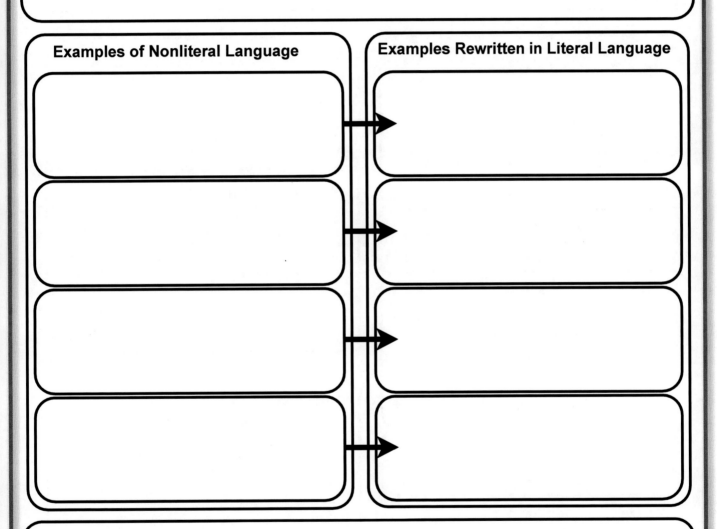

Examples of Nonliteral Language   **Examples Rewritten in Literal Language**

Write your own example of figurative language and its literal counterpart.

_____

_____

Name:_____ **Date:** _____

Directions: Choose a poem to read. Retell the story or events by referring to terms such as stanza, scene, or chapter. Describe how each successive part builds on earlier sections.

Assessment

Poem:_____

Author:_____

Stanza _____ tells about...

_____

_____

_____

How does the next part build on the earlier section?

_____

_____

_____

Stanza _____ tells about...

_____

_____

_____

How does the next part build on the earlier section?

_____

_____

_____

Stanza _____ tells about...

_____

_____

_____

Name:_____ **Date:**_____

Directions: Choose a story to read. Think about the point of view of the main character during an event in the story. Is your point of view the same as the character's? Explain your thinking and why your point of view agrees or disagrees with the character's.

Assessment

Story:_____

Author:_____

Character: _____

Character Description:_____

_____

_____

Event from the story:

_____

_____

_____

_____

Character's Point of View	**My Point of View**
_____	_____
_____	_____
_____	_____
_____	_____

Name:_____ **Date:** _____

Directions: Choose a story to read. Study one of the illustrations and describe what you see. Explain how different aspects of the illustration contributes to the words of the story. How does it create mood or emphasize aspects of a character or setting?

Assessment

Story:_____

Author:_____

Illustrator: _____

**Illustration
Description:**_____

_____

_____

_____

Contribution:_____

_____

_____

_____

_____

_____

_____

_____

_____

Name:_____ **Date:** _____

Directions: Choose two different stories to read by the same author and featuring the same character. Compare and contrast the theme, setting, and plot of each story.

Assessment

Author:_____

Story 1:_____

Story 2:_____

Character:_____

Theme:_____

Theme:_____

Setting:_____

Setting:_____

Plot:_____

Plot:_____

Score _____

Name: _____ **Date:** _____

Directions: After a year of reading different kinds of literature, choose your favorite story, drama, and poem to summarize.

Assessment

Favorite Story: _____

Written By: _____

Summary: _____

_____

_____

_____

Favorite Drama: _____

Written By: _____

Summary: _____

_____

_____

_____

Favorite Poem: _____

Written By: _____

Summary: _____

_____

_____

_____

Name:_____   **Date:**_____

Directions: Choose a grade-level text to read. Ask 3 questions that can be answered by reading the text. Provide responses to the questions, citing evidence from the text.

Assessment

Text:_____

Author:_____

Q 1:_____

_____

A 1:_____

_____

Q 2:_____

_____

A 2:_____

_____

Q 3:_____

_____

A 3:_____

_____

Name:_____   **Date:** _____

Directions: Determine the main idea of an informational text you choose. Recount the key details and explain how they support the main idea.

Assessment

Text:_____

Author:_____

Main Idea

_____
_____
_____

Key Detail

_____
_____

Key Detail

_____
_____

Key Detail

_____
_____

Name: _____ **Date:** _____

Directions: When reading informational text, be aware of the relationship between the events that take place. One event may cause the effect of another. Record such events on the graphic organizer below. Then summarize.

Assessment

Story: _____

Subject: _____

Author: _____

Event

_____
_____
_____
_____

Event

_____
_____
_____
_____

Event

_____
_____
_____
_____

Event

_____
_____
_____
_____

Summary

_____
_____
_____
_____

Name: _____   **Date:** _____

Directions: When reading informational text, be aware of the content words you will find. These academic and domain-specific words and phrases may be new to you. Use context clues, or a reference source, to find meanings of content words in your text.

Assessment

Story: _____

Subject: _____

Author: _____

content word or phrase

_____

meaning

_____

_____

content word or phrase

_____

meaning

_____

_____

content word or phrase

_____

meaning

_____

_____

Name:_____   **Date:**_____

Directions: Choose a topic to research. Use text features and search tools to locate information. Record the information and circle the type of tool you used.

Assessment

Topic:_____

information	source

information

heading   graph
caption   photo
index   diagram
contents   chart
sidebar   cutaway
hyperlink   menu

information

heading   graph
caption   photo
index   diagram
contents   chart
sidebar   cutaway
hyperlink   menu

information

heading   graph
caption   photo
index   diagram
contents   chart
sidebar   cutaway
hyperlink   menu

information

heading   graph
caption   photo
index   diagram
contents   chart
sidebar   cutaway
hyperlink   menu

Name: _____ **Date:** _____

Directions: Choose an informational text to read on a particular topic. What is the author's point-of-view? What is your point-of-view? Tell the major similarity and difference between both points-of-view.

Assessment

Text: _____

Topic: _____

Author: _____

Author's Point of View on Topic

_____
_____
_____
_____
_____

My Point of View on Topic

_____
_____
_____
_____
_____

Major Similarity

_____
_____
_____
_____

Major Difference

_____
_____
_____
_____

Name:_____   **Date:** _____

Directions: Choose an informational text to read on a particular topic. Observe an illustration used in the text. Describe the illustration and explain how it helps you understand the text.

Assessment

Text: _____

Topic: _____

Author:_____

Describe the illustration. Is it a photo? Drawing? Diagram?

How does the illustration help you understand the text?

Something the illustration tells me.

Something the illustration implies.

Name:_____   **Date:** _____

Directions: When we read we find connections between sentences and paragraphs that help us to understand the text. Readers make comparisons, locate examples of cause and effect, and follow sequence. Choose an informational story to read. Cite examples of connections you find and explain how they help you better understand the text.

Assessment

Text: _____

Topic: _____

Author: _____

I found a connection between...

_____ **and** _____

This connection helped me better understand the text because…

_____

_____

I found a connection between...

_____ **and** _____

This connection helped me better understand the text because…

_____

_____

I found a connection between...

_____ **and** _____

This connection helped me better understand the text because…

_____

_____

Third Grade Common Core Assessment

Name: _____   **Date:** _____

Directions: Read two different texts about the same topic or event. Compare and contrast the details of both texts.

Assessment

Topic or Event: _____

Text 1: _____

Author: _____

Text 2: _____

Author: _____

Similarity: _____

_____

_____

Similarity: _____

_____

_____

Difference: _____

_____

_____

Difference: _____

_____

_____

Name:_____ **Date:** _____

Directions: After a year of reading different kinds of informational text, choose your favorite science text, history text, and biography to summarize and show your understanding.

Assessment

Favorite Science Text: _____

Written By: _____

Summary: _____

_____

_____

Favorite History Text: _____

Written By: _____

Summary: _____

_____

_____

Favorite Biography Text: _____

Written By: _____

Summary: _____

_____

_____

Name:_____   Date: _____

Directions: Read the clues below to decipher a word based on the meaning and the suffix. Figure out the word or words that fit the clues.

Assessment A

WORD	AFFIX	MEANING
	-less	does not cease
	mis-	to understand incorrectly
	-ly	done without noise
	-less	has no use
	un-	not safe
	-er	has more speed
	re-	construct again
	pre-	to purchase in advance

Directions: Read the words below. Figure out the suffix in each one. Then write a meaning in your own words.

WORD	SUFFIX	MEANING
digestible		
frailty		
information		
flexible		
amazement		
similarity		
humidify		
likable		

Name: _____   **Date:** _____

Directions: Read the multi-syllable words below aloud to a partner. Write the number of syllables in the column next to the word. If you read the word correctly, color the star. What do you think the word means? How do you know? Discuss.

Assessment B

Multi-syllable Word	Syllable Count	Read Right?	Multi-syllable Word	Syllable Count	Read Right?
fortitude		☆	enticing		☆
posture		☆	irritability		☆
multiplication		☆	prehistoric		☆
environment		☆	indistinguishable		☆
supercilious		☆	superficiality		☆

Read the irregularly-spelled words below aloud to a partner. If you read the word correctly, color the star. what do you think the word means? How do you know? Discuss.

irregularly-spelled word		irregularly-spelled word	
bologna	☆	could	☆
circuit	☆	height	☆
enough	☆	knee	☆
friends	☆	journey	☆
country	☆	father	☆

Name:_____   **Date:** _____

Directions: Read grade-level prose and poetry with accuracy, appropriate rate, and understanding.

Assessment

Title:_____

Level:_____ Shows comprehension:_____

Error Rate: Total Words:_____ / Errors:_____ ER = 1:_____

Self Correction Rate: Total Errors + Total SC / Total SC: _____ = 1:_____

Accuracy Rate: (Total Words - Total Errors)/Total words x 100 = _____ %

Rate of Fluency: Total WPM _____   Total Errors: _____ WCPM: _____

Retelling: _____

_____

Areas of concern: _____

_____

  Student comprehends reading.

  Student read most words correctly.

  Student read with expression.

  Student self-corrected most errors.

  Student used context to guess a word(s).

Name:_____   **Date:** _____

Directions: Read grade-level prose and poetry with accuracy, appropriate rate, and understanding.

Assessment - Instructions

Running Record

As the student reads aloud a benchmark text, keep track of the errors and self-corrections the student makes.

•√ correct words
•record errors by writing the *replacement* or *skipped* word above the actual word
•write *R* when the child repeats a word or phrase
•write *SC* above any word or phrase that is self-corrected
•tick off the errors and self corrections (SC) to the right of the text using tallies ///
•add the errors and self-corrections
•use these totals to calculate the error rate, accuracy rate, and self-correction rate

Calculate the error rate
The error rate is expressed as a ratio and is calculated by using this formula:
Total words / Total errors = Error rate
(ex: 100/4 = 25   ER = 1:25) {student read 25 words correctly for every one error made}

Calculate the accuracy rate
The accuracy rate is expressed as a percentage. You calculate the accuracy rate using this formula:
[Total words read - Total errors] / Total words read x 100 = Accuracy rate
(ex: [100-4]/100 x 100 = 96 AR = 96%)

Accuracy Rate Chart
Independent: 95% - 100%
Instructional: 90% - 94%
Frustrational: 89% and below

Calculate the self-correction rate
The self-correction rate is expressed as a ratio and can be calculated by using this formula:
(Number of errors + Number of self corrections) / Number of self corrections = SC rate
(ex: [4 + 6]/6 = 1.67 or 2 (round to nearest whole number) SC = 1:2) {student self-corrects 1 out of every 2 words}

Fluency

Using a passage that is a fluency benchmark, or is appropriately leveled, the student will read for one minute. Tally the number of errors, not the type of error. Encourage the student to read as many words as possible and not treat this as a running record by going back and rereading.

Calculate the number of WPM (Words Per Minute) - Errors = WCPM (Words Correct Per Minute)
Use this standard rate chart to score.

Grade 1 ... 80 wcpm		Grade 4 ... 140 wcpm	
Grade 2 ... 90 wcpm		Grade 5 ... 150 wcpm	
Grade 3 ... 110 wcpm		Grade 6 ... 180 wcpm	

Name: _____   **Date:** _____

Directions: Write an opinion piece about a current event. Provide reasons and explain how these reasons support your opinion. Write a concluding statement.

Assessment - Page 1

Current Event Summary: _____

_____

_____

_____

_____

_____

My Opinion: _____

_____

_____

_____

_____

_____

_____

_____

_____

_____

Name: _____   **Date:** _____

Directions: Write an opinion piece about a current event. Provide reasons and explain how these reasons support your opinion. Write a concluding statement.

Assessment - Page 2

Reason #1
_____
_____
_____
_____
_____

Reason #2
_____
_____
_____
_____
_____

Reason #3
_____
_____
_____
_____
_____

Reason #4
_____
_____
_____
_____
_____

Conclusion:
_____
_____

Name:_____   **Date:**_____

Directions: Use this page to write a draft, using the two planning sheets for notes.

Assessment - Page 3

_____

_____

_____

_____

_____

_____

_____

_____

_____

_____

_____

_____

_____

_____

_____

_____

_____

_____

_____

_____

Name: _____   **Date:** _____

Directions: Write an informative text that examines a topic. Provide details, facts, definitions, and a concluding statement. Use this organizer to collect your information, then write your text, grouping related information. Provide illustrations if needed to enhance comprehension.

Assessment - Page 1

Topic: _____
_____
_____

Facts: _____

_____

_____

_____

_____

_____

_____

Definitions:

_____   _____

_____   _____

_____   _____

_____   _____

Name: _____   **Date:** _____

Directions: Write an informative text that examines a topic. Provide details, facts, definitions, and a concluding statement. Use this organizer to collect your information, then write your text, grouping related information. Provide illustrations if needed to enhance comprehension.

Assessment - Page 2

Details: _____

_____

_____

_____

Illustrations may aid comprehension. What kinds of illustrations might be helpful for this text?

_____

_____

_____

_____

_____

_____

Concluding Statement: _____

_____

_____

_____

Name: _____   **Date:** _____

Directions: Write a draft here, using pages 1 and 2 as a planner.

Assessment - Page 3

_____

_____

_____

_____

_____

_____

_____

_____

_____

_____

_____

_____

_____

_____

_____

Score _____

Name: _____   **Date:** _____

Directions: Write a narrative, real or imaginary, which includes events described with detail and clear sequence. Establish a situation or setting, with a narrator or characters, and include dialogue and descriptions of actions, thoughts, and feelings. Include a strong closing statement. Use the organizer below to prepare your narrative.

Assessment - Page 1

My Story: _____

_____

Real or imagined? _____

Event: _____

_____

Event: _____

_____

Detail: _____

_____

_____

_____

_____

Detail: _____

_____

_____

_____

_____

Characters: _____

_____

Dialogue: _____

_____

_____

_____

Third Grade Common Core Assessment

© http://CoreCommonStandards.com

Name:_____ **Date:** _____

Directions: Write a narrative, real or imaginary, which includes events described with detail and clear sequence. Establish a situation or setting, with a narrator or characters, and include dialogue and descriptions of actions, thoughts, and feelings. Include a strong closing statement. Use the organizer below to prepare your narrative.

Assessment - Page 2

Event: _____

_____

Event: _____

_____

Detail: _____

_____

_____

_____

Detail: _____

_____

_____

_____

Characters: _____

_____

Dialogue: _____

_____

_____

_____

Closing: _____

_____

_____

Name:_____   **Date:** _____

Directions: Write a draft here, using pages 1 and 2 as a planner.

Assessment - Page 3

_____

_____

_____

_____

_____

_____

_____

_____

_____

_____

_____

_____

_____

_____

_____

_____

Name:_____ **Date:** _____

Directions: Create and analyze a piece of writing that shows what you have learned this year. Your writing should show development, detail, and organization. Tell the genre in which you wrote and share your writing with a peer.

Assessment - Page 1

Title: _____

Genre: _____ Topic: _____

_____
_____
_____
_____
_____
_____
_____
_____
_____
_____
_____
_____
_____
_____
_____

Name:_____   **Date:**_____

Directions: Create and analyze a piece of writing that shows what you have learned this year. Your writing should show development, detail, and organization. Tell the genre in which you wrote and share your writing with a peer.

Assessment - Page 2

Name:_____ **Date:**_____

Directions: With guidance and support from peers and adults, students should be able to demonstrate their skills in developing and strengthening writing as needed by planing, revising, and editing. Teachers and peers can use this checklist to asses student writing.

Assessment

☐   1. The beginning grabs (or hooks) the reader's attention.

☐   2. Student answers a variety of questions within the writing. Who? What? Where? When? Why? How?

☐   3. Student uses enough detail to express feelings and thoughts.

☐   4. Student adds details, reasons, or examples.

☐   5. Student uses descriptive words so the reader can better comprehend.

☐   6. Student uses varied sentence beginnings.

☐   7. Student uses figurative language such as similes, metaphors, vivid verbs, onomatopoeia, and adjectives.

☐   8. The student uses sentences that stay focused on the topic.

☐   9. The student's writing flows sequentially.

☐   10. The ending brings the piece to a close.

Name:_____ **Date:** _____

Directions: Use this checklist to record what digital skills you are able to perform.

Assessment

Digital Skill	Date	Success
I can use a mouse well. (double-click; move cursor to desired place; scroll if available.)		
I know where all common characters are on the keyboard.		
I know how to use the space bar; back space; delete; and return.		
I can open and close different programs.		
I can change the font and size of the font.		
I can add a graphic to a document.		
I can drag and drop an item.		
I can copy/paste an item.		
I can save a file.		
I can print work.		
I can create a Powerpoint Presentation.		
I can locate information on the Internet.		
I can send an email.		
I can attach a file to an email.		

Third Grade Common Core Assessment © http://CoreCommonStandards.com

Name: _____   **Date:** _____

Directions: Conduct a research project that builds knowledge about a topic.

Assessment

My question: _____

_____

The resources I will use:

- ☐ encyclopedia
- ☐ biography
- ☐ magazine
- ☐ journal
- ☐ book
- ☐ newspaper article

- ☐ website
- ☐ interview
- ☐ TV program
- ☐ observation
- ☐ experiment
- ☐ other: _____

How I will present my information:

- ☐ written
- ☐ video
- ☐ 3D model
- ☐ skit
- ☐ powerpoint

- ☐ other: _____
  _____

I will include the following in my writing and/or presentation:

- ☐ video
- ☐ illustrations
- ☐ 3D model
- ☐ diagrams
- ☐ charts/graphs
- ☐ music

- ☐ posters
- ☐ power point
- ☐ oral presentation
- ☐ acting
- ☐ other: _____

Name: _____   **Date:** _____

Directions: Gather information from print and digital sources about a topic. Take notes and sort into categories.

Assessment - Page 1

Topic: _____

_____

Information: _____   **Source:** _____

_____   _____

_____   _____

Information: _____   **Source:** _____

_____   _____

_____   _____

Information: _____   **Source:** _____

_____   _____

_____   _____

Information: _____   **Source:** _____

_____   _____

_____   _____

Name: _____   **Date:** _____

Directions: Gather information from print and digital sources about a topic. Take notes and sort into categories.

Assessment - Page 2

Sort your information into categories.

Category: _____

Information: _____

_____

_____

_____

_____

_____

_____

Category: _____

Information: _____

_____

_____

_____

_____

_____

_____

Score ⬭

Name: _____   **Date:** _____

Directions: Use this checklist to record the types of writing you create.

Assessment

Writing Genre	Date	Audience	Purpose
Journal Entry			
Scientific Research Paper			
Historical Research paper			
Biography			
Autobiography			
Poem			
Song			
Adventure Story			
Realistic Fiction			
Nonfiction Story			
Informational Writing			
Procedural Writing			
Interview			
News Story			
Letter			

Name: _____   **Date:** _____

Directions: Engage effectively in a range of collaborative discussions.   Use this organizer to take notes of others' ideas, build upon them, and express your own clearly.

Assessment

I came to the discussion prepared.	☆	I asked meaningful questions.	☆
I was respectful of others' ideas.	☆	I stayed on topic.	☆
I listened when others talked.	☆	I offered ideas and suggestions.	☆
I responded when I was asked a question.	☆	I gained the floor in a respectful way.	☆

What others are saying...

_____

_____

_____

My thoughts...

_____

_____

_____

What I learned from this discussion...

_____

_____

_____

Name:_____   **Date:** _____

Directions: Choose a scientific journal article or historical article to read. Determine the main idea of the article and write the supporting details you find.

Assessment

Source: _____

Author: _____

Date of article: _____   Topic: _____

Main Idea

_____

_____

_____

Supporting Detail	**Supporting Detail**	**Supporting Detail**
_____	_____	_____
_____	_____	_____
_____	_____	_____

Summary

_____

_____

_____

Name:_____   **Date: _____**

Directions: Listen to a guest speaker who is visiting your school or class, or watch a speaker online discuss a particular topic.   Ask open and closed questions to gain information. Record any answers in your own words.

Assessment

Questioning takes practice. Asking the right question is important in gathering the information needed.

Types of questions:
Closed Question: A closed question usually receives a short, factual answer. For example, "Are you hot?" The answer could be "Yes," or "No." Or, "Where is the Church?" An address may be the answer.

Open Questions: Open questions usually receive longer, more detailed answers. These questions usually begin with *why, what*, or *how*. The open questions asks the respondent for his or her knowledge, opinions, or feelings. Asking for someone to describe some idea or topic is also way of asking an open question.

1. ☐   **OPEN QUESTION** ☐   **CLOSED QUESTION** *(check one)*

QUESTION: _____

_____

ANSWER: _____

_____

2. ☐   **OPEN QUESTION** ☐   **CLOSED QUESTION** *(check one)*

QUESTION: _____

_____

ANSWER: _____

_____

3. ☐   **OPEN QUESTION** ☐   **CLOSED QUESTION** *(check one)*

QUESTION: _____

_____

ANSWER: _____

_____

Score

Name:_____ **Date:**_____

Directions: Storytelling is a skill and tradition that has been passed on for generations. Before humans started writing, experiences were shared orally.

Assessment

Reflect upon an experience that you have had in the past. Recount your experience with appropriate facts and relevant, descriptive details. Speak clearly at an understandable pace. You can practice this skill by recording yourself and listening to how you sound.

SUMMARY: _____
_____
_____
_____

IMPORTANT FACTS:
_____
_____
_____
_____
_____
_____

IMPORTANT DETAILS:
_____
_____
_____
_____
_____
_____

FEELINGS TO SHARE:
_____
_____
_____
_____
_____

KEY WORDS TO USE:
_____
_____
_____
_____
_____

Name:_____   **Date:** _____

Directions: Create an engaging audio recording of a poem or story.   Use a computer, iPod, iPad, or digital recorder to record your voice. Use fluid reading and speak with interest in order to express, emphasize, or enhance certain facts or details. Don't forget to include your own point of view. Share your recording with another person.

Assessment

The story I will read for my recording is _____.

It was written by _____.

The story is about _____.

Components I will add to make my presentation better...

_____ computer graphics	_____ songs
_____ scanned photographs	_____ drawings
_____ scanned drawings	_____ music
_____ computer drawings	_____ sound effects
_____ poster	_____ microphone
_____ movie/TV clips	_____ video

Reflection:

What I liked about my audio presentation:_____

_____

What I can improve upon in my audio presentation:_____

_____

Comments from my peers:_____

_____

Name: _____   **Date:** _____

Directions: Read the tasks below. Explain each task aloud to a classmate or teacher. Be sure to speak in complete sentences and provide detail. Have your partner rate your use of complete, detailed sentences.

Assessment A

☆ Rate 1-5 stars.   1 Star = Few complete sentences and not much detail.
5 stars = All complete sentences and lots of relevant detail.

Task 1: Explain how to give a dog a bath.

Task 2: Explain the difference between a caterpillar and a worm.

Task 3: Explain why it is important to obey road safety rules when walking, or riding a bike.

Name:_____   **Date:** _____

Directions: Your teacher will give you 3 tasks. Explain each task aloud to a classmate or teacher. Be sure to speak in complete sentences and provide detail. Have your partner rate your use of complete, detailed sentences.

Assessment B

 Rate 1-5 stars.

1 Star = Few complete sentences and not much detail.
5 stars = All complete sentences and lots of relevant detail.

Task 1: _____

Task 2: _____

Task 3: _____

Name: _____   Date: _____

Directions: Write an example of each part of speech in the gray boxes. On the lines below, create sentences using the given part of speech. and then explain its function in the sentence.

Assessment A

NOUN: _____

SENTENCE: _____

_____

FUNCTION: _____

PRONOUN: _____

SENTENCE: _____

_____

FUNCTION: _____

ADJECTIVE: _____

SENTENCE: _____

_____

FUNCTION: _____

ADVERB: _____

SENTENCE: _____

_____

FUNCTION: _____

Name:_____ **Date:** _____

Directions: Create simple, compound, and complex sentences for each task in the grey boxes. The grey boxes for numbers 1-4 require you to write the proper word first, and then write the sentences.

Assessment B

1. plural of **flower:** _____

Use in a **Simple Sentence:** _____.

2. plural of **woman:** _____

Use in a **Simple Sentence:** _____.

3. past tense of **shout:** _____

Use in a **Compound Sentence:** _____

_____.

4. past tense of **bring:** _____

Use in a **Compound Sentence:** _____

_____.

5. coordinating conjunction: **yet**

Use in a **Complex Sentence:** _____

_____.

6. coordinating conjunction: **although**

Use in a **Complex Sentence:** _____

_____.

Name: _____   **Date:** _____

Directions: Change each adjective below to a comparative or superlative adjective. Change each present tense verb to future or past tense. Write a sentence for each.

Assessment C

1. ROOT: warm   COMPARATIVE: _____   SUPERLATIVE: _____

COMPARATIVE: _____

SUPERLATIVE: _____

2. ROOT: kind   COMPARATIVE: _____   SUPERLATIVE: _____

COMPARATIVE: _____

SUPERLATIVE: _____

3. ROOT: tall   COMPARATIVE: _____   SUPERLATIVE: _____

COMPARATIVE: _____

SUPERLATIVE: _____

4. PRESENT: play   PAST: _____   FUTURE: _____

PAST TENSE: _____

FUTURE TENSE: _____

5. PRESENT: walk   PAST: _____   FUTURE: _____

PAST TENSE: _____

FUTURE TENSE: _____

6. PRESENT: sting   PAST: _____   FUTURE: _____

PAST TENSE: _____

FUTURE TENSE: _____

Third Grade Common Core Assessment   © http://CoreCommonStandards.com

Name:_____   **Date:** _____

Directions: Choose two pieces of schoolwork that contain writing you completed. (Example: journal entries, published writing, short answer worksheets, essays, or letters.) Check your work for evidence of command of the conventions including capitalization, punctuation, and spelling.

Assessment

Fictional Work: _____

Date Written:_____ Rating: ☆☆☆☆☆			
Capitalized titles.		Formed and used possessives.	
Used commas in addresses and dates.		Spelled words correctly.	
Used commas in dialogue.		Added suffixes and prefixes correctly.	
Used quotation marks in dialogue.		Used reference materials to check and correct spellings.	

What do I still need to work on? _____

Nonfiction Work: _____

Date Written:_____ Rating: ☆☆☆☆☆			
Capitalized titles.		Formed and used possessives.	
Used commas in addresses and dates.		Spelled words correctly.	
Used commas in dialogue.		Added suffixes and prefixes correctly.	
Used quotation marks in dialogue.		Used reference materials to check and correct spellings.	

What do I still need to work on? _____

Score _____

Name: _____   **Date:** _____

Directions: Follow and recognize proper language rules when speaking, writing, reading, and listening. Write where you would find examples of each type of language.

Assessment

formal writing	informal writing	formal speaking	informal speaking

Directions: Read the texts below. Thinking about the word choice and conventions used, write whether the text is formal spoken, formal written, informal spoken, or informal written.

"Wow! That song is so totally awesome! Who sings it?"

_____

"I thoroughly enjoyed that musical piece. What is the name of the musical group that sings the song?"

_____

Dear Sue,
Could you please collect my purse? I believe it is on the table. Thank you.

_____

hey grab my lunch bag
its on my bed
thx! :)   ttl

_____

Score

Name: _____   **Date:** _____

Directions: Choose an informational text to read. Record key words from the text and use sentence context to define the words. Write the meaning of the word and the sentence clues you used.

Assessment A

Title: _____

Author: _____

word	meaning	sentence clues

Name: _____ **Date:** _____

Directions: Read the word on the left. Add the affix (prefix or suffix) provided. Write the meaning of the new word.

Assessment B

word	affix	new word	meaning
due	over-	_____	
marine	sub-	_____	
mouth	-ful	_____	
cycle	uni-	_____	
scope	tele-	_____	
talented	multi-	_____	
sister	-hood	_____	
pedal	bi-	_____	
date	post-	_____	
heart	-less	_____	

Name:_____   **Date:**_____

Directions: Choose a story to read. Find examples of figurative phrases and write the literal meaning of each.

Assessment A

Story:_____

Author:_____

figurative phrase	what i think the literal meaning is

Directions: Choose two examples of figurative language from above. Write a real-life connection for each.

figurative phrase	real-life examples of how this phrase might be used

Name: _____   Date: _____

Directions: Choose a word that describes a state of mind or degree of certainty. Write other words that are related to the original word. Example: knew, believed, suspected, heard, wondered. Explain how the meanings are different, and then use each synonym in a sentence.

Assessment B

MY WORD: [   ]

SYNONYM	How is the meaning different?
[ ]	[ ]

Example sentence:

SYNONYM	How is the meaning different?
[ ]	[ ]

Example sentence:

SYNONYM	How is the meaning different?
[ ]	[ ]

Example sentence:

SYNONYM	How is the meaning different?
[ ]	[ ]

Example sentence:

Name:_____   **Date:** _____

Directions: When you read different texts, record some of the conversational, academic and domain-specific vocabulary words and phrases that you find. Try to accurately use these words in general conversation or in sentences.

Assessment

Text:_____ Word:_____

Sentence:_____

_____

Text:_____ Word:_____

Sentence:_____

_____

Text:_____ Word:_____

Sentence:_____

_____

Text:_____ Word:_____

Sentence:_____

_____

Text:_____ Word:_____

Sentence:_____

_____

Common Core
State Standards

Math Assessments

Grade 3

- **Math Standards**
- **English Standards**

**Worksheets and Activities
that teach every standard!**

Name: _____   **Date:** _____

Directions: For the multiplication equations below, use the suggested solving method for each column. The first one in each column has been done for you.

Assessment

SOLVE WITH ARRAYS	REPEATED ADDITION	NUMBER STORIES
SAMPLE: **2 X 6** **This array shows 12.**	*SAMPLE:* **2 X 6** **2 + 2 + 2 + 2 + 2 + 2 = 12**	*SAMPLE:* **2 X 6** **I had two boxes. Each box had 6 leaves inside. How many leaves did I have?** **Answer = 12 leaves**
9 X 3	5 X 3	7 X 2
8 X 1	4 X 6	8 X 6
6 X 6	3 X 7	5 X 9

Name: _____   **Date:** _____

Directions: For the division equations below, use the suggested solving method for each column. The first one in each column has been done for you.

Assessment

EQUAL SHARES	DRAW A PICTURE	NUMBER STORIES
SAMPLE: **15 ÷ 3**	*SAMPLE:* **15 ÷ 3**	*SAMPLE:* **15 ÷ 3**
These equal shares show 15.	XX XXX XX XXX XX XXX 3 sets of 5.	Mom baked 15 meatballs. There were 3 plates. How many meatballs did each plate get? Answer = 5 meatballs
8 ÷ 2	12 ÷ 3	10 ÷ 2
9 ÷ 3	24 ÷ 6	36 ÷ 6
50 ÷ 5	27 ÷ 9	14 ÷ 2

64

Name: _____   **Date:** _____

Directions: Solve the multiplication problems. You may use drawings and equations to show your work.

Assessment A

Clive placed 12 boxes on the ground. He threw bouncy balls into the boxes. Each box had 5 bouncy balls. How many bouncy balls were there all together?

_____ bouncy balls

For the class play, Mrs. Potter had us place the seats into 9 rows. Each row had 8 seats. How many seats were there in all?

_____ seats

My brother built some towers yesterday with his blocks. He built 7 tall towers. Each tower had 14 blocks. How many blocks did my brother use?

_____ blocks

Grandma planted some flowers in her garden. She planted 4 types of flowers. Each type of flower was in its own pot. Each pot had 12 flowers. How many flowers did Grandma plant?

_____ flowers

I collect spiders. Right now I have 11 spiders in a jar. How many legs are there?

_____ spider legs

Name: _____   **Date:** _____

Directions: Solve the division problems. You may use drawings and equations to show your work.

Assessment B

Kyle had 20 pieces of candy left in his bag. His mom divided them equally among Kyle and his 4 friends. How many pieces of candy did each child get?

_____ pieces

Dad bought 90 candles yesterday. The candles were in boxes. Each box had 10 candles. How many boxes did dad buy?

_____ boxes

Silvio invited me and some friends over for pizza. He had 3 pizzas delivered. The pizzas were cut into a total of 30 slices. Each person got 6 slices. How many people ate pizza?

_____ people

Susie drew 4 flowers with petals. She drew a total of 56 petals. Each flower had the same amount of petals. How many petals were on each flower?

_____ petals

**When Pops visited, he brought a dozen donuts. I had to share them with my 3 brothers. We each got the same amount. How many donuts did we get to eat?

_____ donuts

Score

Name: _____ **Date:** _____

Directions: Read the equations below. What missing number makes each equation true? Write the missing numbers into the equations.

Assessment

1. $24 \div \boxed{} = 8$

2. $12 \times 3 = \boxed{}$

3. $55 \div 5 = \boxed{}$

4. $4 \times \boxed{} = 28$

5. $\boxed{} \div 6 = 8$

6. $13 \times 3 = \boxed{}$

7. $72 \div \boxed{} = 6$

8. $\boxed{} \times 7 = 35$

9. $81 \div 9 = \boxed{}$

10. $9 \times 7 = \boxed{}$

Name:_____   **Date:**_____

Directions: Solve the multiplication equations by using one of the strategies you have learned.

Assessment

6x4=24 so 4x6=24 (commutative)   3x5x2 is 3x5=15 and 15x2=30 (associative)

8x7 is 8x(5+2) so (8x5) + (8x2) = 40 + 16 which is 56..so 8x7=56 (distributive)

1. 3 x 6 =

I used the _____ property.

2. 3 x 5 x 9 =

I used the _____ property.

3. 13 x 5 =

I used the _____ property.

4. 2 x 10 x 3 =

I used the _____ property.

5. 4 x 4 x 4 =

I used the _____ property.

Name: _____ Date: _____

Directions: Solve the division problems by solving its corresponding multiplication fact.

Assessment

1. $32 \div 8 =$ _____

$8 \times$ _____ $= 32$

6. $28 \div 4 =$ _____

$4 \times$ _____ $= 28$

2. $45 \div 9 =$ _____

$9 \times$ _____ $= 45$

7. $81 \div 9 =$ _____

$9 \times$ _____ $= 81$

3. $36 \div 3 =$ _____

$3 \times$ _____ $= 36$

8. $15 \div 3 =$ _____

$3 \times$ _____ $= 15$

4. $72 \div 8 =$ _____

$8 \times$ _____ $= 72$

9. $77 \div 7 =$ _____

$7 \times$ _____ $= 77$

5. $25 \div 5 =$ _____

$5 \times$ _____ $= 25$

10. $60 \div 5 =$ _____

$5 \times$ _____ $= 60$

Name: _____ **Date:** _____

Directions: Fluently multiply and divide the numbers within 100. Check your work with a calculator or have someone else check your work when you are done. Color a star for each correct answer.

Assessment

1.

20 x 4 = _____

2.

45 x 2 = _____

3.

12 x 5 = _____

4.

33 x 2 = _____

5.

15 x 6 = _____

6.

50 ÷ 5 = _____

7.

84 ÷ 6 = _____

8.

72 ÷ 2 = _____

9.

56 ÷ 4 = _____

10.

39 ÷ 3 = _____

Third Grade Common Core Assessment

Name:_____   **Date:** _____

Directions: Solve the following problems. Think about the operation (+, - , x , ÷) you can use to solve each problem.
Write an equation to help you solve. Place a letter in the space of the unknown quantity. ex: 45 ÷ a = 9

Assessment

1.

Patrick has 44 marbles. Spencer has 36.   How many more marbles does Patrick have than Spencer?

_____ marbles

If Patrick and Spencer combine their marbles into one group and split them equally in half, how many marbles would each child get?

_____ marbles

2.

Jean bought 3 watermelons for the class.   Each watermelon was cut into 10 slices.   If each of the 24 students takes a slice, how many slices will be left over?

_____ slices

If the extra slices are shared equally between Mrs. Popper and Mr. Snell, how many will each teacher get?

_____ slices

3.

The sporting goods store just received a new shipment of bikes.   There are 10 red bikes, 13 blue bikes, and 27 gray bikes. How many bikes arrived in total?

_____ bikes

If half of the bikes go out onto the sales floor, and half stay in the back, how many bikes will be out on the floor?

_____ bikes

4.

Stella has 4 times as many pencils as Judy.   Judy has 12 pencils.   How many pencils does Stella have?

_____ pencils

They combined their pencils together and divided them equally among 5 boxes.   How many pencils were in each box?

_____ pencils

Score

Name: _____   **Date:** _____

Directions: Look for the patterns in the addition/subtraction IN/OUT boxes below. Complete each box by following the pattern. Write the rule for each IN/OUT box.

Assessment A

1.

rule	in	out
	9	19
	6	16
	17	
	20	
	38	

2.

rule	in	out
	30	45
	52	67
		82
	29	
		86

3.

rule	in	out
	22	19
	43	40
	68	
	55	
	97	

4.

rule	in	out
	77	65
	36	24
		52
	88	
		12

5.

rule	in	out
	38	
		76
	45	65
		24
	40	

6.

rule	in	out
	56	
	78	
		42
	32	16
		0

Third Grade Common Core Assessment

© http://CoreCommonStandards.com

Name: _____   **Date:** _____

Directions: Look for the patterns in the multiplication/division IN/OUT boxes below. Complete each box by following the pattern. Write the rule for each IN/OUT box.

Assessment B

1.

rule	in	out
	5	25
	11	55
	7	
	14	
	30	

2.

rule	in	out
	6	54
	9	81
		90
	12	
		36

3.

rule	in	out
	46	23
	74	37
	90	
	88	
	52	

4.

rule	in	out
	48	16
	33	11
		22
	96	
		12

5.

rule	in	out
	3	
		60
	4	48
		72
	10	

6.

rule	in	out
	63	
	90	
		0
	81	9
		2

Third Grade Common Core Assessment

© http://CoreCommonStandards.com

73

Name: _____ **Date:** _____

Directions: Round each number to its nearest ten or hundred.

Assessment

1. Round to the nearest ten.

   47

2. Round to the nearest hundred.

   568

3. Round to the nearest ten.

   94

4. Round to the nearest hundred.

   202

5. Round to the nearest ten.

   39

6. Round to the nearest hundred.

   616

7. Round to the nearest ten.

   352

8. Round to the nearest hundred.

   481

9. Round to the nearest ten.

   411

10. Round to the nearest hundred.

    965

Name:_____   **Date:** _____

Directions: Fluently add and subtract within 1000. Solve the problems below. Use a calculator or have someone else check your work when you have completed all of the problems. Color a star for each correct answer.

Assessment

1. 329
   + 611

6. 832
   + 100

2. 456
   - 244

7. 925
   - 741

3. 626
   + 155

8. 756
   + 121

4. 433
   - 330

9. 781
   - 233

5. 192
   + 580

10. 580
    + 217

Third Grade Common Core Assessment

© http://CoreCommonStandards.com

Name: _____   **Date:** _____

Directions: Multiply the whole numbers below by multiples of ten. Use a calculator or have someone else check your work when you have completed all of the problems. Color a star for each correct answer.

Assessment

1.
```
    70
x    5
_____
```

6.
```
    20
x    9
_____
```

2.
```
    80
x    3
_____
```

7.
```
    40
x    8
_____
```

3.
```
    50
x    4
_____
```

8.
```
    10
x    5
_____
```

4.
```
    60
x    2
_____
```

9.
```
    30
x    9
_____
```

5.
```
    80
x    3
_____
```

10.
```
    50
x    8
_____
```

Third Grade Common Core Assessment   © http://CoreCommonStandards.com

Score

Name: _____   Date: _____

Directions: The shapes below have been divided into equal parts.   Write the fraction that represents the shaded part of the whole shape.

Assessment

1.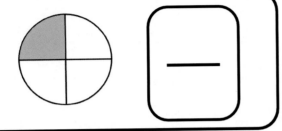

6.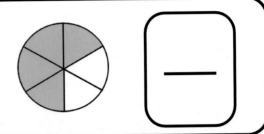

2.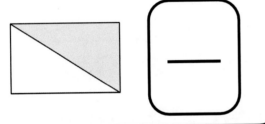

7.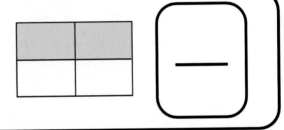

3.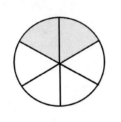

8.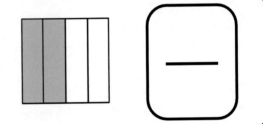

4.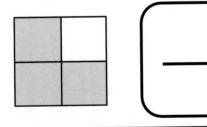

9.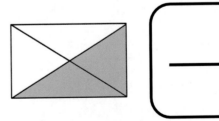

5.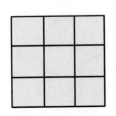

10.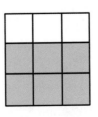

Score

Name:_____ **Date:** _____

Directions: The number lines below have been divided into equal parts. Write the fraction that represents where the dot falls on each line.

Assessment A

1.

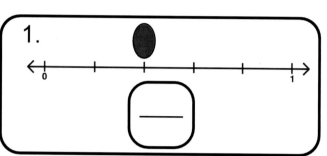

6.

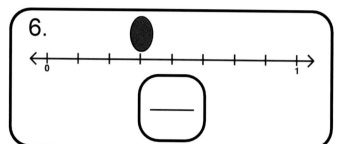

2.

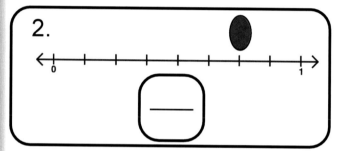

7.

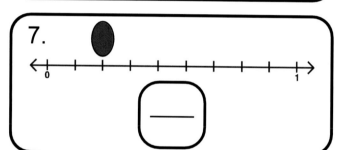

3.

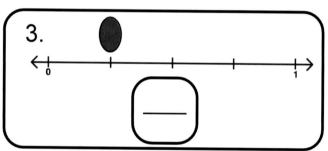

8.

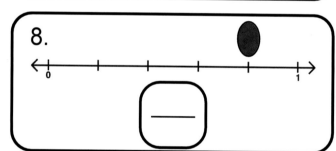

4.

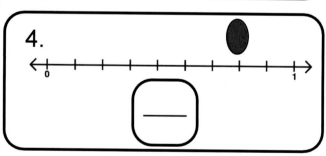

9.

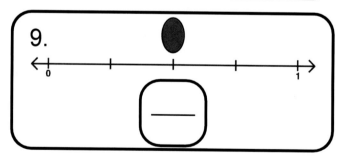

5.

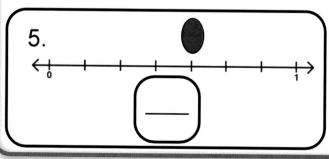

10.

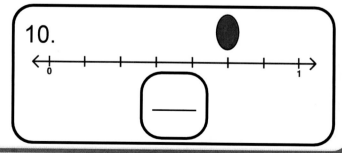

Name: _____   **Date:** _____

Directions: Divide the number lines below into equal parts based on the fraction shown. Draw a dot where the fraction would be found on the number line.

Assessment B

1.   2/8

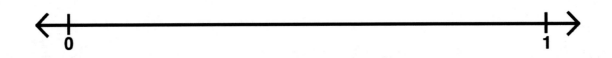

2.   5/6

3.   3/10

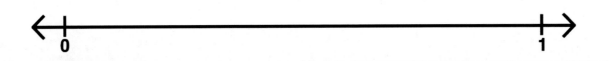

4.   7/9

5.   1/4

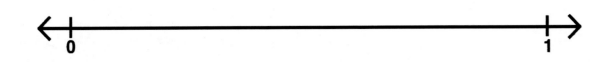

Name: _____ **Date:** _____

Directions: Look at the partitioned shapes below. Are the fractions the same for each pair? Check the box for same or different for each pair.

Assessment A

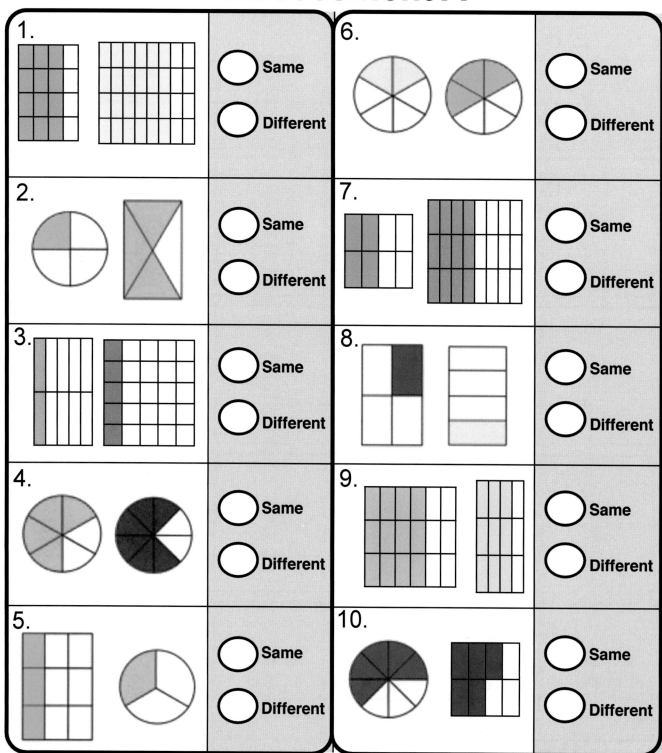

1. ◯ Same ◯ Different

6. ◯ Same ◯ Different

2. ◯ Same ◯ Different

7. ◯ Same ◯ Different

3. ◯ Same ◯ Different

8. ◯ Same ◯ Different

4. ◯ Same ◯ Different

9. ◯ Same ◯ Different

5. ◯ Same ◯ Different

10. ◯ Same ◯ Different

Name:_____   **Date:** _____

Directions: Read the fractions below. Write an equivalent fraction for each. Then, explain why they are equivalent.

Assessment B

$$\frac{3}{4} \underline{}$$

$$\frac{2}{6} \underline{}$$

$$\frac{4}{5} \underline{}$$

$$\frac{3}{8} \underline{}$$

$$\frac{1}{2} \underline{}$$

Score [   ]

Name: _____   Date: _____

Directions: Express the equivalent whole number fraction for each shape below.

Assessment C

1.

5.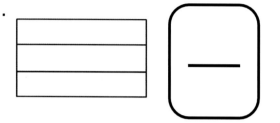

2.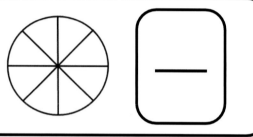

6.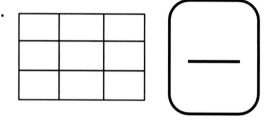

3.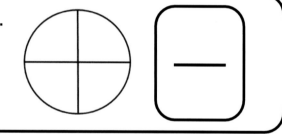

7.

4.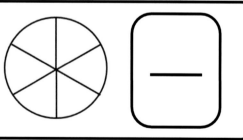

8.

Directions: Write the equivalent whole number fraction for each number line.

9. 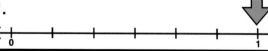   ——

10. 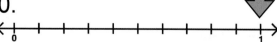   ——

Third Grade Common Core Assessment

Name: _____ Date: _____

Directions: Compare the fractions below. Write <, >, or = to compare, knowing that each fraction compared below refers to the same whole.

Assessment D

1. $\dfrac{5}{6}$ ⬚ $\dfrac{10}{12}$

2. $\dfrac{8}{36}$ ⬚ $\dfrac{4}{18}$

3. $\dfrac{3}{5}$ ⬚ $\dfrac{3}{9}$

4. $\dfrac{1}{8}$ ⬚ $\dfrac{1}{6}$

5. $\dfrac{6}{12}$ ⬚ $\dfrac{4}{12}$

6. $\dfrac{4}{16}$ ⬚ $\dfrac{2}{4}$

7. $\dfrac{2}{6}$ ⬚ $\dfrac{1}{3}$

8. $\dfrac{4}{8}$ ⬚ $\dfrac{20}{40}$

9. $\dfrac{5}{20}$ ⬚ $\dfrac{3}{4}$

10. $\dfrac{6}{9}$ ⬚ $\dfrac{3}{5}$

Score _____

Name: _____ **Date:** _____

Directions: Read the number stories below. Calculate the elapsed time for each story.

Assessment

1. Juliet read her Harry Potter book for an hour and 15 minutes.

   What time did Juliet begin reading? __ : __ __

   What time did Juliet finish reading? __ : __ __

   start

2. Carlos woke up an hour late today. He was supposed to wake up at 4:30 a.m., but instead his clock looked like this:

   What time did Carlos wake up? __ : __ __
   How long did Carlos oversleep? __ : __ __

3. Sandra started watching her favorite movie at this time. She shut off the TV at 2:16.

   What time did Sandra start her movie? __ : __ __
   How long did Sandra watch TV? __ : __ __

   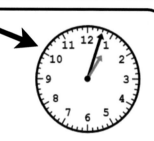

4. It takes mom 1 hour and 11 minutes minutes to drive to work. If she wants to be at work by 9:00 a.m., at what time does she need to leave the house?

   __ : __ __

   leave

   arrive

5. Candace started baking at noon. She spent 1 hour and 13 minutes making cupcakes and 45 minutes making a cake.

   When were the cupcakes done? __ : __ __
   What time did she finish baking? __ : __ __

   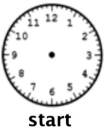
   start

   finish

Third Grade Common Core Assessment

Score

Name: _____ Date: _____

Directions: Circle the best measurement unit (liters, milliliters, grams, or kilograms) for each object listed below. Then, solve the number stories using some of these units of measure.

Assessment

1. **the volume of a bottle of soda** grams kilograms liters milliliters	4. **the weight of a handful of sand** grams kilograms liters milliliters	7. **the volume of a tureen of soup** grams kilograms liters milliliters
2. **the weight of a full suitcase** grams kilograms liters milliliters	5. **the volume of a swimming pool** grams kilograms liters milliliters	8. **the weight of a small bird** grams kilograms liters milliliters
3. **the volume of a teaspoon of medicine** grams kilograms liters milliliters	6. **the weight of a box of lead** grams kilograms liters milliliters	9. **the volume of a bottle of nail polish** grams kilograms liters milliliters

10. Steve needed to bake 3 cakes for a party. He followed the recipe for one cake and multiplied by 3 to increase the ingredients. The recipe called for 60 grams of white flour. How many grams of white flour was needed for 3 cakes?

_____ grams

11. Jane's dog weighed 30 kg. Pete's dog weighed 14 kg. John's dog weighed 2 times as much as Pete's dog. How much did all three dogs weigh together?

_____ kilograms

12. Paula and Pam brought 22 two-liter bottles of cream soda to the conference. Sean and Sam brought 13 two-liter bottles of orange soda. How many liters of soda were available to drink at the conference?

_____ liters

Name:_____   **Date:** _____

Directions: Read the problem below. Create a pictograph that will represent the data. Answer the questions by using the graph.

Assessment

Harriet and her four friends, Lucy, Sally, Patty, and Marcy, collected stickers. They preserved their stickers in books that held 50 stickers each. Below are the number of books each girl had.

Harriet - 6 books   Sally - 4 books   Patty - 6 1/2 books

Lucy - 8 books   Marcy - 2 books

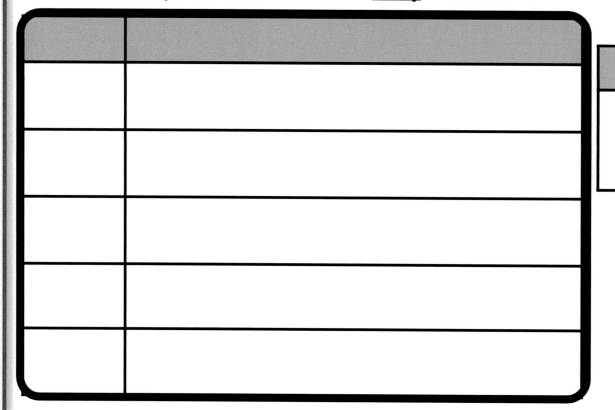

	KEY

1. How many stickers did Harriet collect?

2. How many more stickers did Lucy collect than Marcy?

3. How many stickers were collected in all?

4. How many stickers did Sally and Patty collect altogether?

Name: _____ **Date:** _____

Directions: Measure the length of 6 objects to the nearest inch, half-inch, or quarter-inch. Record the measurements below. Arrange the data to be displayed in the line plot, where the horizontal scale is marked off in appropriate units - whole numbers, halves, or quarters.

Assessment

	Object	Measurement (inches)
1		
2		
3		
4		
5		
6		

Score

Name: _____ **Date:** _____

Directions: Determine the area of the shapes by counting the units in each.

Assessment A

1.

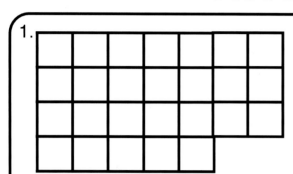

_____ sq units

2.

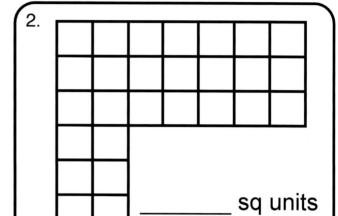

_____ sq units

3.

_____ sq units

4.

_____ sq units

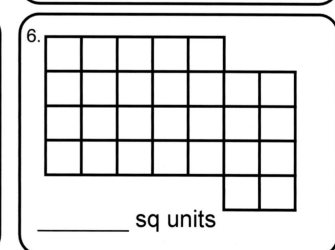

5.

_____ sq units

6.

_____ sq units

Third Grade Common Core Assessment © http://CoreCommonStandards.com

Name:_____　**Date:**_____

Directions: Determine the area of the rectangle below by using centimeter cubes.

Assessment B

A

The area of rectangle A is
_____ sq. cm.

_____ cm X _____ cm = _____ sq. cm

B

The area of rectangle B is
_____ sq. cm.

_____ cm X _____ cm = _____ sq. cm

C

The area of rectangle C is
_____ sq. cm.

_____ cm X _____ cm = _____ sq. cm

Name: _____ **Date:** _____

Directions: Determine the area of each object below. Think about in what unit the area would be measured. Choose the correct unit for each.

Assessment

1.   **section of a map**

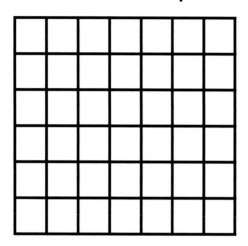

area = _____
sq. cm
sq. mm
sq. miles

2.   **tile floor in classroom**

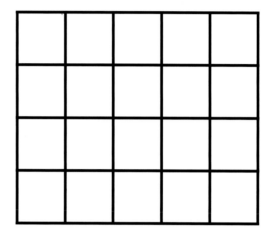

area = _____
sq. in
sq. mm
sq. ft

3.   **tile counter in bathroom**

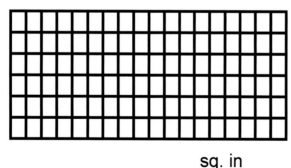

area = _____
sq. in
sq. ft
sq. yds

4.   **floor area in large closet**

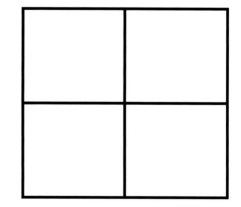

area = _____
sq. m
sq. ft
sq. miles

Name:_____ **Date:** _____

Directions: Determine the area of each shape below. Find the measurement of the sides for questions 1 and 2. Find the area for each shape by multiplying the sides.

Assessment A

1.

_____

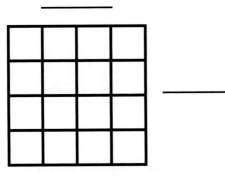

_____

_____ x _____ = _____

Area = _____ sq. units

2.

_____

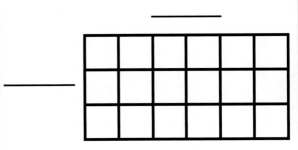

_____

_____ x _____ = _____

Area = _____ sq. units

3.

14

4

_____ x _____ = _____

Area = _____ sq. units

4.

11

23

_____ x _____ = _____

Area = _____ sq. units

Name:_____   **Date:** _____

Directions: Determine the area of each shape below by using the appropriate operations. Hints have been added to #1 and #2.

Assessment B

1.

17

17   **A**   **B**   8

7

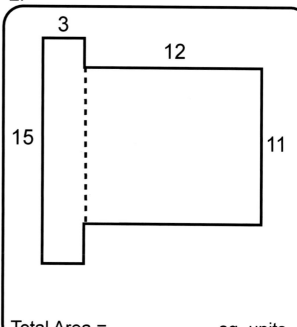

Area of A = _____ sq. units

Area of B = _____ sq. units

Total Area = _____ sq. units

2.

3

12

15   11

Total Area = _____ sq. units

3.

20

5

6

10

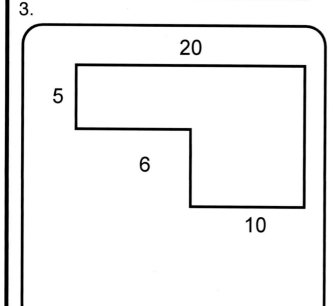

Total Area = _____ sq. units

4.

15

4

6

9

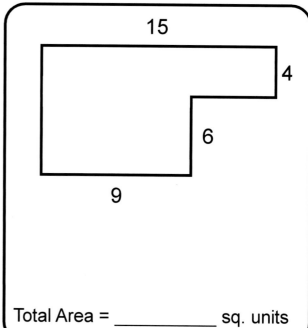

Total Area = _____ sq. units

Score

Name: _____   **Date:** _____

Directions: Determine the area of each shape below by using the distributive property; area of a rectangle with side lengths *a* and *b + c* is the sum of *a x b* and *a x c*. Solve each problem with both methods.

Assessment C

1.

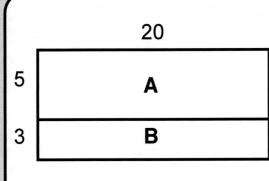

SOLVE USING ADDITION:
Length of A + B = _____
Length of (A+B) x Height = _____
Total Area = _____ sq. units

SOLVE USING MULTIPLICATION:
Area of A = _____ sq. units.
Area of B = _____ sq. units
Total Area of A+B = _____ sq. units

2.

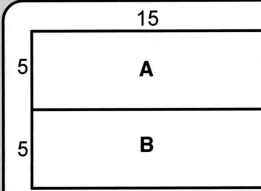

SOLVE USING ADDITION:
Height of A + B = _____
Length x Height of (A+B) = _____
Total Area = _____ sq. units

SOLVE USING MULTIPLICATION:
Area of A = _____ sq. units.
Area of B = _____ sq. units
Total Area of A+B = _____ sq. units

3.

SOLVE USING ADDITION:
Height of A + B = _____
Length x Height of (A+B) = _____
Total Area = _____ sq. units

SOLVE USING MULTIPLICATION:
Area of A = _____ sq. units.
Area of B = _____ sq. units
Total Area of A+B = _____ sq. units

Third Grade Common Core Assessment

© http://CoreCommonStandards.com

Name: _____ **Date:** _____

Directions: Solve the perimeter problems. Use drawings or equations to solve.

Assessment

Mrs. Luis wants to build a fence around her backyard. She measured each side of her yard which is shaped like a pentagon. Side A was 14 ft. Side B was 12 ft. Side C was 10 ft. Sides D and E equaled 25 feet together. How much fencing does Mrs. Luis need to buy?

_____ feet

Bob is adding a chair rail to his living room walls. The four walls total 72 ft. Wall one is 20 ft long. Wall 2 is 16 ft. Wall three is equal to wall one. What is the length of wall 4?

_____ feet

Mr. Plimpton walks the perimeter of our school each morning. The north side of the school is 52 meters. The west side is 47 meters. The school is a rectangle. How many meters does Mr. Plimpton walk each morning?

_____ meters

Sean's thumb nail is a perfect square. One day he decided to find the perimeter of his nail. He measured one side and the result was 12mm. What is the perimeter of Sean's thumb nail? *If Sean's thumb nails are exactly the same, what would the combined perimeter be of both?

_____ mm   * _____mm

The police officer had to secure the perimeter of a house. He used bright yellow police tape in four long sections. Two of the sides were each 45 feet long. A third side was 23 feet long. The total length of tape was 140 feet. How long was the tape on fourth side?

_____ feet

Score _____

Name: _____ Date: _____

Directions: Answer the questions about quadrilaterals and draw examples of quadrilaterals and non-quadrilaterals.

Assessment

What Makes a Quadrilateral?

1. How many sides does a quadrilateral have? _____

2. How many angles does a quadrilateral have? _____

3. Can a quadrilateral have any curved sides? _____

4. Does a quadrilateral have to be an open or closed shape? _____

5. Can a quadrilateral have right angles? _____

6. Does it have to have right angles? _____

Examples of Quadrilaterals:

Examples of Non-Quadrilaterals:

Third Grade Common Core Assessment

95

Name: _____   **Date:** _____

Directions: Partition each shape below into equal parts based on the fraction shown. Center points have been added to help you divide the shapes into fractions. Express the area of each part as a fraction.

Assessment

1.

fourths

NUMERATOR:
DENOMINATOR:

2.

eighths

NUMERATOR:
DENOMINATOR:

3.

thirds

NUMERATOR:
DENOMINATOR:

4.

sixths

NUMERATOR:
DENOMINATOR:

Third Grade Common Core Assessment   © http://CoreCommonStandards.com

3

Common Core State Standards

Progress Reports

Grade 3

- **Math Standards**
- **English Standards**

Worksheets and Activities
that teach every standard!

NAME: _____

Use this form to keep track of progress and grades.

Standard	Grade
RL.3.1	/ 6
RL.3.2 1 & 2	/ 6
RL.3.3	/ 8
RL.3.4	/ 10
RL.3.5	/ 5
RL.3.6	/ 8
RL.3.7	/ 6
RL.3.9	/ 8
RL.3.10	/ 6

Standard	Grade
RI.3.1	/ 6
RI.3.2	/ 8
RI.3.3	/ 6
RI.3.4	/ 6
RI.3.5	/ 8
RI.3.6	/ 8
RI.3.7	/ 8
RI.3.8	/ 6
RI.3.9	/ 8
RI.3.10	/ 6

Standard	Grade
RF.3.3 A	/ 24
RF.3.3 B	/ 30
RF.3.4	/ 5

Standard	Grade
W.3.1 1,2,3	/ 20
W.3.2 1,2,3	/ 20
W.3.3 1,2,3	/ 20
W.3.4 1 & 2	/ 10
W.3.5	/ 10
W.3.6	/ 14
W.3.7	/ 6
W.3.8 1 & 2	/ 10
W.3.10	/ 15

Standard	Grade
SL.3.1	/ 14
SL.3.2	/ 10
SL.3.3	/ 9
SL.3.4	/ 10
SL.3.5	/ 6
SL.3.6 A	/ 15
SL.3.6 B	/ 15

Standard	Grade
L.3.1 A	/ 12
L.3.1 B	/ 10
L.3.1 C	/ 24
L.3.2	/ 10
L.3.3	/ 16
L.3.4 A	/ 18
L.3.4 B	/ 20
L.3.5 A	/ 12
L.3.5 B	/ 12
L.3.6	/ 15

NOTES:

NAME: _____

Use this form to keep track of progress and grades.

Standard	Grade
3.OA.1	/ 18
3.OA.2	/ 18
3.OA.3 A	/ 5
3.OA.3 B	/ 5
3.OA.4	/ 10
3.OA.5	/ 5
3.OA.6	/ 10
3.OA.7	/ 10
3.OA.8	/ 8
3.OA.9 A	/ 26
3.OA.9 B	/ 26

Standard	Grade
3.NF.1	/ 10
3.NF.2 A	/ 10
3.NF.2 B	/ 5
3.NF.3 A	/ 10
3.NF.3 B	/ 10
3.NF.3 C	/ 10
3.NF.3 D	/ 10

Standard	Grade
3.MD.1	/ 14
3.MD.2	/ 12
3.MD.3	/ 9
3.MD.4	/ 10
3.MD.5 A	/ 6
3.MD.5 B	/ 12
3.MD.6	/ 8
3.MD.7 A	/ 20
3.MD.7 B	/ 12
3.MD.7 C	/ 12
3.MD.8	/ 6

Standard	Grade
3.NBT.1	/ 10
3.NBT.2	/ 10
3.NBT.3	/ 10

Standard	Grade
3.G.1	/ 12
3.G.2	/ 8

NOTES:

3

Common Core State Standards

Blank Progress Reports

Grade 3

- **Math Standards**
- **English Standards**

Worksheets and Activities
that teach every standard!

100

NAME: _____

Use this form to keep track of progress and grades.

Standard	Grade
RL.3.1	
RL.3.2 1 & 2	
RL.3.3	
RL.3.4	
RL.3.5	
RL.3.6	
RL.3.7	
RL.3.9	
RL.3.10	

Standard	Grade
RI.3.1	
RI.3.2	
RI.3.3	
RI.3.4	
RI.3.5	
RI.3.6	
RI.3.7	
RI.3.8	
RI.3.9	
RI.3.10	

Standard	Grade
RF.3.3 A	
RF.3.3 B	
RF.3.4	

Standard	Grade
W.3.1 1,2,3	
W.3.2 1,2,3	
W.3.3 1,2,3	
W.3.4 1 & 2	
W.3.5	
W.3.6	
W.3.7	
W.3.8 1 & 2	
W.3.10	

Standard	Grade
SL.3.1	
SL.3.2	
SL.3.3	
SL.3.4	
SL.3.5	
SL.3.6 A	
SL.3.6 B	

Standard	Grade
L.3.1 A	
L.3.1 B	
L.3.1 C	
L.3.2	
L.3.3	
L.3.4 A	
L.3.4 B	
L.3.5 A	
L.3.5 B	
L.3.6	

NOTES:

Third Grade Common Core Assessment Workbook

NAME: _____

Use this form to keep track of progress and grades.

Standard	Grade
3.OA.1	
3.OA.2	
3.OA.3 A	
3.OA.3 B	
3.OA.4	
3.OA.5	
3.OA.6	
3.OA.7	
3.OA.8	
3.OA.9 A	
3.OA.9 B	

Standard	Grade
3.NF.1	
3.NF.2 A	
3.NF.2 B	
3.NF.3 A	
3.NF.3 B	
3.NF.3 C	
3.NF.3 D	

Standard	Grade
3.MD.1	
3.MD.2	
3.MD.3	
3.MD.4	
3.MD.5 A	
3.MD.5 B	
3.MD.6	
3.MD.7 A	
3.MD.7 B	
3.MD.7 C	
3.MD.8	

Standard	Grade
3.NBT.1	
3.NBT.2	
3.NBT.3	

Standard	Grade
3.G.1	
3.G.2	

NOTES:

Common Core State Standards

3

English Answer Keys

Grade 3

- **Math Standards**
- **English Standards**

Worksheets and Activities that teach every standard!

103

Reading: Literature

RL.3.1 Assessment

Responses may vary but should include three questions answered with evidence form the text.

RL.3.2 Assessment - Pages 1 & 2

This form can be used with any fable, myth or folktale. The answers are included for 'The Ant and the Grasshopper'

Title: The Ant and the Grasshopper
Message: It is wise to worry about tomorrow today.
Details: The ant collected food while the grasshopper laughed at her. The ant continued to work, but the grasshopper played and danced and sang.
When the grasshopper was cold and hungry, it had no food. The ant was prepared.

RL.3.3 Assessment

Responses may vary. Responses should include a description of a character and how the character's actions contribute to an event in the story.

RL.3.4 Assessment

Responses may vary but should include examples of figurative language and their literal counterparts.

RL.3.5 Assessment

Responses may vary but should include a retelling of the poem and how the stanzas build on one another.

RL.3.6 Assessment

Responses may vary but should include the main character's point of view and the student's point of view.

RL.3.7 Assessment

Responses may vary but should include a description of one of the illustrations and how it contributes to the text.

RL.3.9 Assessment

Answers will vary, but should accurately compare two stories in the following areas: Characters, Settings, Problems, and Solutions.

RL.3.10 Assessment

Students may use this record sheet to record their reading in appropriate grade-level books and poems in various genres and styles. They should have a brief summary written with correct grammar and punctuation.

RI.3.1 Assessment

Responses may vary but should include three questions answered with evidence form the text.

RI.3.2 Assessment

Responses may vary but should include the main idea of the story with supporting key details.

RI.3.3 Assessment

Responses may vary but should include text events and a summary.

RI.3.4 Assessment

Responses may vary but should include various content words or phrases and their meanings.

RI.3.5 Assessment

Responses may vary but should include various information and the source used to acquire it.

RI.3.6 Assessment

Responses may vary but should include the points-of-view of the author and the students with a comparison between the two.

RI.3.7 Assessment

Responses may vary but should include a description of an illustration used in the text and how it helps the reader better understand the text.

RI.3.8 Assessment

Responses may vary but should include connections the student made while reading text.

RI.3.9 Assessment

Responses may vary but should compare and contrast the details of two different texts on the same topic.

RI.3.10 Assessment

Students may use this record sheet to record their reading in appropriate grade-level books and texts in various genres and styles. They should have a brief summary written with correct grammar and punctuation.

Reading: Foundational Skills

RF.3.3 Assessment A

TOP SECTION:

ceaseless (endless)
misunderstand (miscomprehend, misconstrue)
quietly (noiselessly)
useless
unsafe
faster, quicker (speedier, swifter, fleeter)
rebuild (reconstruct)
prepurchase, prepay

BOTTOM SECTION:

word	suffix	meaning
digestible	-ible	to be able to digest
frailty	-ty	to be frail
information	-tion	something to learn/know
flexible	-ible	to be able to bend
amazement	-ment	feeling amazed
similarity	-ty	to be similar
humidify	-fy	to make humid
likable	-able	something you can like

RF.3.3 Assessment B

TOP SECTION:

fortitude (3)   enticing (3)
posture (2)   irritability (6)
multiplication (5)   prehistoric (4)
environment (4)   indistinguishable (6)
supercilious (5)   superficiality (7)

For both sections check pronunications.

RF.3.4 Assessment

Use the form and the directions on the following page to check for reading accuracy and comprehension. Keep a running record of each student's reading progress.

Writing

W.3.1 Assessment - Pages 1, 2, & 3

Responses may vary but should include an event summary with the writer's opinion. Opinion should be supported by reasons and evidence.

Pages 1 & 2 are planners for a draft on page 3.

W.3.2 Assessment - Pages 1, 2, & 3

Responses may vary but should include information on a topic with details, facts, definitions, and a concluding statement. Pages 1 & 2 are planners for a draft on page 3.

W.3.3 Assessment - Pages 1, 2, & 3

Responses may vary but should be in the form of a narrative which includes events described in detail and has clear sequence, dialogue, character development, and a closing.

Pages 1 & 2 are planners for a draft on page 3.

W.3.4 Assessment - Pages 1 & 2

Responses may vary but should be an original piece of writing that shows the student's growth in writing.

W.3.5 Assessment

Responses may vary. Checklist can be used by students and teachers to assess writing growth.

W.3.6 Assessment

Responses may vary. Checklist can be used by students and teachers to assess knowledge in digital learning.

W.3.7 Assessment

Responses may vary. Checklist can be used by students to plan a research project and by teachers to analyze how well the student planned and executed the project.

W.3.8 - Pages 1 & 2

Responses may vary. Form can be used by students to gather information about a topic and by teachers to analyze how well the student collected and categorized the information.

W.3.10

Responses may vary. Form can be used by students and /or to record the types of writing the students complete over the course of the year.

Speaking and Listening

SL.3.1 Assessment

Responses may vary. Students and/or teachers can use the checklist to record student participation in collaborative groups.

SL.3.2 Assessment

Responses may vary but should include the main idea of a scientific or historical article, supporting details, and a summary.

SL.3.3 Assessment

Responses may vary but should include various types of questions and accurate answers. Open and closed questions should be identified correctly by the check boxes.

SL.3.4 Assessment

Responses may vary but should include a short summary of a personal experience, facts, details, and other information that will enhance oral storytelling.

SL.3.5 Assessment

Responses may vary but should include information that helps to plan recording of an oral reading or storytelling.

SL.3.6 Assessment A

Responses may vary. Oral explanations should include complete, detailed sentences and students should speak clearly as they explain how to accomplish the tasks.

SL.3.6 Assessment B

Responses may vary. Oral explanations should include complete, detailed sentences and students should speak clearly as they explain how to accomplish the tasks.

Language

L.3.1 Assessment A

Sentences and words chosen will vary. The functions of the words should be similar to the following examples:

Noun: names a person, place, thing, idea, or animal
Pronoun: Takes the place of a noun in the sentence.
Adjective: describes a noun in the sentence
Adverb: describes a verb in the sentence

L.3.1 Assessment B

Sentence responses will vary, but the words in the gray boxes should be:
1. flowers
2. women
3. shouted
4. brought

L.3.1 Assessment C

Sentence responses will vary, but the words in the gray boxes should be:
1. warmer, warmest
2. kinder, kindest
3. taller, tallest
4. played, will play
5. walked, will walk
6. stung, will sting

L.3.2 Assessment

Students should use this form to check over their work in fictional and nonfictional writing. Teachers can also use it for an assessment of a final draft.

L.3.3 Assessment

TOP SECTION:
Responses will vary. Check for accuracy.

BOTTOM SECTION:

informal spoken	formal spoken
formal written	informal written

L.3.4 Assessment A

Answers will vary depending on text and words chosen.

L.3.4 Assessment B

NEW WORD:	MEANING:
overdue	past due
submarine	underwater
mouthful	filled the mouth
unicycle	one-wheeled cycle
telescope	long-distance look
sisterhood	association of sisters
bipedal	two-footed
postdate	date after the fact
heartless	without feeling

L.3.5 Assessment A

Answers will vary, but should indicate examples of figurative language. The bottom section should also feature examples of how to use this figurative language in everyday speech.

L.3.5 Assessment B

Answers will vary. Synonyms should be words that fit the original word, if in varying degrees. The differences in meanings should be explained, and then an example sentence should be used.

L.3.6 Assessment

Answers will vary. Vocabulary chosen should be properly used in sentences, either original or from the texts they were located in.

Common Core State Standards

Math Answer Keys

Grade 3

- **Math Standards**
- **English Standards**

Worksheets and Activities
that teach every standard!

Operations and Algebraic Thinking

3.OA.1 Assessment

Responses may vary. Answers from left to right by column.

ARRAYS	ADDITION	WORDS
9x3=18	5+5+5=15 or 3+3+3+3+3=15	Ex. I have 7 boxes, each box has 2 things...
8x1=8	6+6+6+6=24 or 4+4+4+4+4+4=24	Ex. I have 8 boxes, each box has 6 things...
6x6=36	3+3+3+3+3+3+3=21 or 7+7+7=21	Ex. I have 5 boxes, each box has 9 things...

3.OA.2 Assessment

Responses may vary. Answers from left to right by column.

SHARES	PICTURES	WORDS
8÷2=4	12÷3=4	10÷2=5
9÷3=3	24÷6=4	36÷6=6
50÷5=10	27÷9=3	14÷2=7

3.OA.3 Assessment A

1. 12 x 5 = 60 balls
2. 9 x 8 = 72 seats
3. 7 x 14 = 98 blocks
4. 4 x 12 = 48 flowers
5. 11 x 8 = 88 spider legs

3.OA.3 Assessment B

1. 20 ÷ 5 (kyle + 4 friends) = 4 pieces
2. 90 ÷ 10 = 9 candles
3. 30 ÷ 6 = 5 people
4. 56 ÷ 4 = 14 petals
5. 12 ÷ 4 = 3 donuts

3.OA.4 Assessment

1. 3
2. 36
3. 11
4. 7
5. 48
6. 39
7. 12
8. 5
9. 9
10. 63

3.OA.5 Assessment

Answers should be as follows with the property used and work shown.

1. 18
2. 135
3. 65
4. 60
5. 64

3.OA.6 Assessment

1. 4,4
2. 5,5
3. 12,12
4. 9,9
5. 5,5
6. 7,7
7. 12
8. 5,5
9. 11,11
10. 12,12

3.OA.7 Assessment

1. 80
2. 90
3. 60
4. 66
5. 90
6. 10
7. 14
8. 36
9. 14
10. 13

3.OA.8 Assessment

1. 8 marbles, 40 marbles
2. 6 slices, 3 slices
3. 50 bikes, 25 bikes
4. 48 pencils, 12 pencils

3.OA.9 Assessment A

1. (+10) 27, 30, 48
2. (+15) 67, 44, 71
3. (-3) 65, 52, 94
4. (-12) 64, 76, 24
5. (+20) 58, 56, 4, 60
6. (-16) 40, 62, 58, 16

3.OA.9 Assessment B

1. (x5) 35, 70, 150
2. (x9) 10, 108, 4
3. (÷2) 45, 44, 26
4. (÷3) 66, 32, 36
5. (x12) 36, 5, 6, 120
6. (÷9) 7, 10, 0, 18

Numbers & Operations in Base Ten

3.NBT.1 Assessment

1. 50
2. 600
3. 90
4. 200
5. 40
6. 600
7. 350
8. 500
9. 410
10. 1000

3.NBT.2 Assessment

1. 940
2. 212
3. 781
4. 103
5. 772
6. 932
7. 184
8. 877
9. 548
10. 797

3.NBT.3 Assessment

1. 350
2. 240
3. 200
4. 120
5. 240
6. 180
7. 320
8. 50
9. 270
10. 400

Numbers & Operations - Fractions

3.NF.1 Assessment

1. 1/4
2. 1/2
3. 2/6 or 1/3
4. 3/4
5. 9/9 or 1 whole

6. 4/6 or 2/3
7. 2/4 or 1/2
8. 2/4 or 1/2
9. 2/4 or 1/2
10. 6/9 or 2/3

3.NF.2 Assessment A

1. 2/5
2. 6/8 or 3/4
3. 1/4
4. 7/9
5. 4/7

6. 3/8
7. 2/9
8. 4/5
9. 2/4 or 1/2
10. 5/7

3.NF.2 Assessment B

Approximate Answers:

1. 2/8

2. 5/6

3. 3/10

4. 7/9

5. 1/4

3.NF.3 Assessment A

1. same
2. different
3. same
4. different
5. same

6. different
7. same
8. same
9. different
10. same

3.NF.3 Assessment B

Responses will vary. Explanations should be accurate. Suggested answers:

1. 6/8 or 9/12
2. 1/3 or 3/9
3. 8/10 or 12/15
4. 6/16 or 9/24
5. 2/4 or 3/6

3.NF.3 Assessment C

1. 2/2
2. 8/8
3. 4/4
4. 6/6

5. 3/3
6. 9/9
7. 5/5
8. 1/1

9. 6/6
10. 10/10

3.NF.3 Assessment D

1. =
2. =
3. >
4. <
5. >

6. <
7. =
8. =
9. <
10. >

Measurement & Data

3.MD.1 Assessment
1. Begin at 3:41, finish at 4:56
2. Woke up at 6:08, overslept by 1 hr 38 min
3. Started at 1:03, watched 1 hr 13 mins
4. leave at 7:49, arrive at 9:00 (check clocks to make sure they match these numbers)
5. cupcakes done at 1:13, baking finished at 1:58. start clock = 12:00, finish clock = 1:58

3.MD.2 Assessment
1. liters   4. grams   7. liters
2. kilograms   5. liters   8. grams
3. milliliters   6. kilograms   9. milliliters

10. 180 grams
11. 30 + 14 + 28 = 72 kilos
12. (22 + 13) x 2 = 70 liters

3.MD.3 Assessment
Make sure the pictograph is filled in properly.
Harriet: @@@@@@
Sally: @@@@
Patty: @@@@@@C (this one has a 1/2)
Lucy: @@@@@@@@
Marcy: @@

1. 50 x 6 = 300
2. (8 - 2) x 50 = 300
3. 300 + 200 + 325 + 400 + 100 = 1325
4. (4 + 6.5) x 50 = 525

3.MD.4 Assessment
Using this page, make sure students properly fill out the data table and graph their measurements properly. All parts of the graph should be properly labeled.

3.MD.5 Assessment A
1. 26 sq units   2. 27 sq units
3. 24 sq units   4. 20 sq units
5. 20 sq units   6. 28 sq units

3.MD.5 Assessment B
A. 20 sq cm   5 x 4 = 20
B. 42 sq cm   7 x 6 = 42
C. 21 sq cm   3 x 7 = 21

3.MD.6 Assessment
1. 42 sq miles   2. 20 sq ft
3. 108 sq. in   4. 4 sq m

3.MD.7 Assessment A
Make sure blanks are filled in appropriately.
1. 4x4 = 16 sq units   2. 3x6=18 sq units
3. 4x14= 56 sq units   4. 23x11= 253 sq un

3.MD.7 Assessment B
Check work. Wrok may vary depending on how the last 2 shapes are split in two.
1. A=17x17=289   B=8x7=56
    Total Area = 345 sq units.
2. A=15x3=45   B=12x11=132
    Total Area = 177 sq units
3. A=20x5=100   B=6x10=60
    Total Area = 160 sq units.
4. A=15x4=60   B=6x9=54
    Total Area = 114 sq units

3.MD.7 Assessment C
Solve each question 2 ways. The answer should be the same either way.
1. addition: 13, 130, 130 sq units
    multiplication: 100, 30, 130 sq units
2. addition: 8, 160, 160 sq units
    multiplication: 100, 60, 160 sq units
3. addition: 10, 150, 150 sq units
    multiplication: 75, 75, 150 sq units

3.MD.8 Assessment
1. 61 feet
2. 35 feet
3. 198 meters
4. 48 mm for one, 96 mm for both
5. 27 feet

Geometry

3.G.1 Assessment

TOP SECTION:

1. 4
2. 4
3. No
4. Closed
5. Yes
6. No

Quadrilaterals:	**Non-Quad.:**
rhombus	triangles
square	hexagons
parallelogram	octagons
rectangle	circles
trapezoid	semicircles
dart	crescents
irregular quadrilateral	pentagons

3.G.2 Assessment

Responses will vary. Make sure each section is partitioned into the proper number of pieces. Each one should have a colored portion, which should be correctly identified in the fraction box.

Common Core State Standards
Educating classrooms one standard at a time.

Terms of Use

Fore more Common Core Standards Posters, Activities, Worksheets, and Workbooks, visit http://CoreCommonStandards.com.

Worksheets created by: Have Fun Teaching
Activities created by: Have Fun Teaching
Posters created by: Have Fun Teaching

Made in the USA
Middletown, DE
29 August 2023

37554467R00071